A Manager's Guide to PR Projects

A Practical Approach

LEA'S COMMUNICATION SERIES
Jennings Bryant/Dolf Zillmann, General Editors

Selected titles in Public Relations (James Grunig, Advisory Editor) include:

Austin / Pinkleton ● Strategic Public Relations Management: Planning and Managing Effective Communication Programs

Culbertson / Chen ● International Public Relations: A Comparative Analysis

Dozier / Grunig / Grunig ● Manager's Guide to Excellence in Public Relations and Communication Management

Fearn-Banks ● Crisis Communications: A Casebook Approach, Second Edition

Grunig ● Excellence in Public Relations and Communication Management

Ledingham / Bruning ● Public Relations as Relationship Management: A Relational Approach to the Study and Practice of Public Relations

Lerbinger ● The Crisis Manager: Facing Risk and Responsibility

---

For a complete list of titles in LEA's Communication Series, please contact Lawrence Erlbaum Associates, Publishers at www.erlbaum.com

A Manager's Guide to PR Projects

A Practical Approach

Patricia J. Parsons
Mount Saint Vincent University

LAWRENCE ERLBAUM ASSOCIATES, PUBLISHERS
2003   Mahwah, New Jersey   London

Camera ready copy for this book was provided by the author.

Lawrence Erlbaum Associates, Inc., Publishers
10 Industrial Avenue
Mahwah, NJ 07430

Cover design by Kathryn Houghtaling Lacey

Library of Congress Cataloging-in-Publication Data

Parsons, Patricia J.
A manager's guide to PR projects : a practical approach /
by Patricia J. Parsons.
        p. cm.
    Includes bibliographical references and index.
    ISBN 0-8058-4547-X (pbk. : alk. paper)
    1. Public relations—Management. I. Title.
    HD59.P355   2003
    659.2—dc21
                                                    2003040857
                                                        CIP

Printed in the United States of America
10 9 8 7 6 5 4 3 2 1

Contents

Contents

A Manager's Guide to PR Projects was conceived, gestated, and produced out of sheer frustration. Perhaps a more academic approach to this explanation would be to say that one university professor experienced considerable difficulty in acquiring appropriate materials to support a pedagogical approach involving student participation and hands-on experience. So she wrote the book herself. But I prefer a less cluttered way of writing and speaking.

For about six years I taught, among other things, a one-semester foundation course in public relations as a professional discipline for our first-year public relations majors, and its follow-up course, that focused primarily on an introduction to the strategic process of public relations planning. Although there is a wide variety of choice in the area of introductory textbooks, and each of them has a chapter or three on strategy, there is far less choice in the search for materials to accompany a first course on communication and public relations planning. There are some excellent communication planning textbooks that provide background and theory, and I use these, but I observed that my students were missing something.

Several years and several hundred student/client public relations plans later, I also found myself in the position of teaching our senior-level course in public relations management. A 4000-level course, it still lacked material of a practical nature for student reading and application. Of course we used James Grunig's "Excellence Study" as well as a variety of case study books over the years, but there was still something missing. Consequently, I set about developing the materials that would be useful for the students. *A Manager's Guide to PR Projects* was the result.

This workbook had its first outing in the fall of 1999 in a prepublication form. I used it for two sections of the 4000-level course, all the while knowing that it was really a more rudimentary book. The student feedback was astoundingly positive and it appeared that they did, indeed, understand the practicalities of the planning process better than their predecessors, and their client work showed it. In addition, I sought feedback from several colleagues and produced the workbook in its final format, which a colleague and I used for several years with good results in terms of the students' ability to take the theory about decision-making and planning and to apply that to real client situations. When the time came for a revised edition, I approached Erlbaum and this book is the result. A departure for any publisher who currently provides materials for public relations education at the postsecondary level, this venture, I believe, shows considerable foresight on the part of this publisher. No one had ever produced a workbook of this kind for public relations. But, in my view, workbooks like this can be truly useful tools for students and practitioners alike.

Preface

A Manager's Guide to PR Projects: A Practical Approach picks up where classic public relations textbooks leave off. It provides hands-on guidance in planning the preliminary research for a public relations project and creating a plan to achieve specific goals, guiding the reader through managing the project's implementation. It contains valuable worksheets that can be used for a visual representation of the planning process for both student edification and presentation to clients.

This is an easy book to read, however, its usefulness to both the student as well as the practitioner is in its focus on guiding the reader during the planning process. This book is a tool: a practical approach.

One caveat: Because this book does provide templates of various kinds, it is easy for the reader to begin to believe that this is the only approach: that the templates are to be followed religiously. This is not the case. Be aware that there are many ways to approach the planning process. This is my recommendation for the beginning practitioner. As experience and judgment develop, individualized, creative approaches to specific client issues will become apparent to the practitioner. Use this workbook as a starting point from which to develop a proactive planning philosophy for public relations and corporate communications.

Please let me know how you have been able to use this book. You can contact me via e-mail at patricia.parsons@msvu.ca.

Patricia J. Parsons APR

Chapter 1

Before We Begin

Vocabulary

- ☐ public relations process

- ☐ systems

- ☐ subsystem

- ☐ input

- ☐ throughput

- ☐ output

- ☐ management

Defining public relations

Public relations has been defined in many ways by many writers and public relations practitioners over the years. How *you* define public relations depends on a number of factors including the following:

- your type of educational background in the field (e.g. journalism, English, marketing, public relations);

- your level of education in PR or related fields (e.g. certificate, bachelor's degree, master's degree);

- the books, magazines, and journals you have read (e.g. PR texts versus marketing texts);

- the professional associations to which you belong (e.g. the International Association of Business Communicators, the Public Relations Association of America, the American Academy of Advertising, the Canadian Public Relations Society) or do not belong;

- your experience in public relations and its related communication fields (e.g. advertising, marketing, graphic design).

There are, however, some important commonalities about how professional public relations in general is defined. This book is based on a number of commonly held beliefs about the practice of public relations.

- ☐ **Public relations is a management function that assists the organization to reach its goals.**

- ☐ **Public relations is a process of research, planning, implementation and evaluation.**

- ☐ **Public relations practice requires both managerial and technical skills, creativity, flexibility and above all, integrity.**

- ☐ **Public relations utilizes targeted communications tools and techniques to help organizations develop and maintain mutually beneficial relationships.**

- ☐ **Public relations can be practiced in for-profit, not-for-profit and governmental venues.**

These beliefs guide the management of public relations projects.

This book is designed as a user-friendly guide to take you through the 4-step public relations planning process from any one of a number of vantage points. You may be a manager, a public relations student, a PR practitioner who needs a review, or someone outside the field who has an interest in public relations planning. Each of you will find something useful and practical in the pages that follow. It is not intended as a crutch, but rather as a learning tool for use both in class and beyond. Its approaches are based on real experiences in the management of communications projects designed to meet organizational goals through achieving public relations objectives.

Using this book

The templates at the end of each chapter are designed to be copied for your personal use as worksheets, and some are even useful as documents that might be shared with a client or employer as appendiceal material in a final written plan.

This workbook presupposes that you are reading, or have read, a variety of supplementary materials that explain in greater detail some of the terms used. There is a vocabulary list at the beginning of each section. These are terms that are used in the text that follows, but that beg fuller explanation toward which the resource list for each chapter will lead you.

Management as a term is a bit like the term "public relations": there are as many definitions as there are managers. Most definitions again, however, have some commonalities. The following are some of those common factors:

Defining management

- Management is a process of getting things done efficiently and effectively.

- Management accomplishes its goals through and with people and the strategic use of other organizational resources, including time and money.

- There are four fundamental activities that managers use to accomplish their goals. These are planning, organizing, leading and controlling.

It's worth noting that these sound a lot like the activities we have already identified as part of the 4-step public relations process – and they are. Thus, for our purposes, the public relations process itself is our fundamental management tool.

Whereas small organizations may have only one main manager, larger organizations – whether for-profit, not-for-profit, or government ventures – tend to have a number of managers. A public relations manager may have a department of one to manage, or a department of many. Every project, however, whether carried out by one person or many, must be planned and managed for it to achieve its goals.

> Modern public relations is a management function that uses a process of research, planning, implementation, and evaluation to help an organization achieve its communication and relationship goals.

Defining "projects"

This book is titled *A Manager's Guide to PR Projects*. Clearly we need a working definition of the term **project** as we are using it in this context. Webster's dictionary defines a project as "something proposed or mapped out in the mind, a course of action; a plan." If we use this definition, a public relations project can be anything from the development of a simple news release (which begins as an idea in someone's mind, is researched, outlined, written, and, at some point, evaluated) up to the most complex strategies for solving organizational problems that stem from external and/or internal relationships. In other words, an excellent public relations practitioner will use a project planning process for everything from the largest to the smallest project, rather than flying by the seat of his or her pants.

As you become more experienced, you begin to realize that you have internalized this process, and simple projects often no longer require a formal, written plan. Sometimes, however, seemingly simple challenges can stump you and you can revert to this useful exercise. More complex strategies always require a written plan using the 4-step process, modified and adapted to the situation at a particular point in the organization's history. This workbook is designed for use in strategic communication planning to achieve public relations objectives.

Public relations process: A few details

Systems theory provides a useful paradigm for examining the relationships between an organization and its publics, and for understanding and applying public relations process.

If we consider the notion that an organization exists within an environment that exerts economic, social, and political pressures on it, we can see that the publics with which that organization interacts are also part of that environment. As such, these publics (whose boundaries the organization defines) are both subject to these same pressures *and* capable of being part of the pressures exerted on the organization.

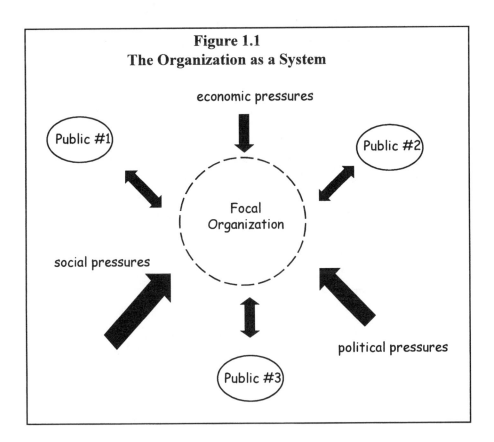

Figure 1.1 illustrates the organization as part of a larger system. Both the organization and its publics are interacting units of the system. Also, note that the arrows from the organization are two-headed, indicating that interaction (communication), in the ideal model, is two-way. This entire workbook assumes that excellent public relations is based on a two-way communication model.

When an organization feels pressures from outside its boundaries (and sometime from inside those same boundaries) it can choose either to maintain the *status quo* or to adapt to the pressures. Maintaining the *status quo* usually results in an organization that is unable to progress and flourish. Adaptation, on the other hand, allows the organization to identify and solve its problems and to capitalize on opportunities (see chapter 2 for more specific definitions of these terms).

If we take a closer look at the focal organization, we can see another system. This system comprises the interacting units that make up the organization itself. The public relations function is one of those units, and it is within this subsystem that the public relations process is carried out. In systems terms, within the public relations function itself, **input** consists of pressures, data, communication from internal or external publics, activities of publics that bring pressure to bear on the organization, and so on. **Throughput** is the public relations process itself (carrying out research, planning, implementing plans, and evaluating plans), and **output** comprises the messages (and how they are carried) to various publics, both internal and external (examples of output include newsletters, videos, events, publicity). Keep in mind that the term "messages" in public relations can mean messages in the literal sense as illustrated by the foregoing examples, but they can also be more implied. For example, it is not just the specific communication activities that make up the organization's output in the public relations process, but its actions as well. In addition, the development or adaptation of policies in response to feedback from important publics can be significant public relations approaches whose messages may appear more subliminal, but are just as key to the development of strong relationships with publics. Thus, two-way communication and the adaptation of the organization to its publics and its environment also constitute outputs.

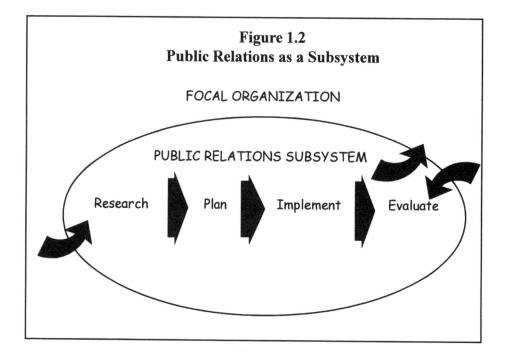

Figure 1.2
Public Relations as a Subsystem

FOCAL ORGANIZATION

PUBLIC RELATIONS SUBSYSTEM

Research   Plan   Implement   Evaluate

These four steps – research, plan, implement, and evaluate – form the basis for what we call public relations process (see Fig. 1.2). This process is nothing more or less than a systematic way to make well-founded, strategic decisions. Furthermore, it is not unique to the field of public relations *per se.* For example, a medical doctor uses a similar process when he or she gathers both subjective and objective information about a patient's condition, determines a diagnosis, decides on a treatment plan, then follows up to determine the outcome, changing the approach, if necessary, based on that outcome. Using that process to deal with the communications issues within an organization is, however, the purview of the public relations profession. Let's examine each step a bit more carefully.

Research: During the research phase, the public relations practitioner gathers information from a variety of sources. These could include such secondary sources as organizational records, governmental statistics, textbooks, or journals. Often, data gathering also includes such primary methods as surveys, interviews, and focus groups.

The communication or public relations audit, which includes both primary and secondary sources for information, is a formalized method of assessing the communication activities of an organization and thus is also a research tool.

Also included in the research phase is analysis. It is not enough simply to gather the information, it must be analyzed so that the problem or opportunity may be identified (more about problems and opportunities in chapter 2).

Plan: The most important aspect of the planning stage is setting objectives for the plan. These are the desired outcomes. Once the objectives are developed, it becomes feasible to look at message development, select channels and vehicles, and determine how, when, and by whom the plan will be implemented.

Implement: During the implementation phase, the plan is carried out. When developing a strategy in the first place, however, the strategist needs to deal with the managing the implementation. How resources will be utilized for execution of the plan is an important part of examining the implementation prior to actually putting the plan into effect.

Evaluate: The final phase is evaluation. The strategist always plans how the project will be evaluated while preparing the initial plan. The evaluation phase itself is really ongoing, although it appears to be the last phase. Evaluation strategies are always developed in direct response to the objectives set for each specific public and the measurement of outcomes is used as research data for future strategies – thus making this a feedback loop and a circular rather than linear process.

Now that we have examined the purpose of this workbook and set our framework for discussing the management of the public relations projects, we'll begin the real work of strategic public relations – creating the strategy.

Onward!

The remainder of this workbook is devoted to the four phases of the public relations process. Each section begins with a listing of important terminology (which you should look up in several theory books if you are unfamiliar with any of them), provides brief background on the step of the process, and then moves quickly to tools that you can use to work through the strategic process.

This is where the creative fun of professional public relations really lies!

Chapter 2

The Research Phase

Vocabulary

- ☐ applied research

- ☐ theoretical research

- ☐ primary research

- ☐ secondary research

- ☐ survey

- ☐ focus group

- ☐ communication audit

- ☐ analysis

- ☐ public relations problem

- ☐ public relations opportunity

An everyday process

Let's presume for a moment that you are sitting at your desk reading this chapter. It's 3 o'clock in the afternoon and you've already had a very busy day. When you got out of bed this morning, you had to get dressed. Look down at what you're wearing right now.

Have you changed your clothes since this morning? If you did, why did you change? Presume for a moment that you are still wearing the same clothes you dressed in when you got up. How did you decide what you would wear today? Getting dressed is an activity that all of us do every day, but we don't usually wear the same clothes (even people who wear uniforms usually have the odd day off from it). How, then, did you decide on the clothes that you now see on yourself?

If you're like most of us, however unconsciously, you gathered a host of data, analyzed it, then made a decision. Eventually, you will evaluate that decision, but let's stick to the data-gathering for a moment more. Here are some of the pieces of data you might have considered before you got dressed.

- What is the weather like?
- What clothes are clean?
- What do I have to do today?
- Who am I likely to see today?
- What kind of impression do I want to make?
- How do I feel today?

Some of the methods you might use to gather answers to these questions are the following:

- Listening to the weather report on the radio
- Looking out the window
- Observing the floor and/or the closet
- Checking your daily appointment book
- Asking a significant other for an opinion

You will analyze all this information, use it to figure out your goal (e.g. to be comfortable, to get that new job, to impress someone special), and then you will create a plan of action. And it's likely that your plan of action will be flawed if you don't gather and analyze this data, resulting in outcomes that you may not like.

You may not be aware of it, but your actions to collect data and analyze it constitute research. So, for our purposes in managing the public relations process, we will use the following definition:

Research is a deliberate, planned, and organized process for collection and analysis of data for the purpose of determining an organization's public relations problems, opportunities, and possible solutions.

What research can accomplish

Let's go back for a moment to your morning decision-making process about your daily wardrobe. Consider this scenario: For several weeks, you have been preparing for a very important job interview that is scheduled for early this morning. You wake up late and giving little thought to what you'll be wearing, you throw on the first thing you see. You arrive at the interview on time, but the receptionist takes one look at you and figures that you must be in the wrong place. You are wearing a rumpled shirt and jacket and you are soaking wet. You hadn't realized that it was raining until it was too late. You have failed to do appropriate and sufficient research, thereby decreasing the likelihood that you will achieve your ultimate goal.

Conducting research before embarking on any kind of public relations venture is critical to its success. For example, before you launch a new employee newsletter to keep them informed, you need to find out what employees need to know, but you also need to determine what employees believe is the most effective and credible way to receive information. If you fail to collect and use this information, you may find yourself with a shiny new newsletter that no one reads, resulting in your inability to achieve your goals, and that costs you money.

On a larger scale, research is crucial to the strategic planning process so that you can answer the following key questions:

- Where are we now?
- Where do we want to go?
- What is likely to be the best route to get there?

Organizations have saved themselves thousands of dollars by conducting research before launching communication campaigns or determining the best way to deal with feedback from publics. For example, what would be the point of trying to change a perceived negative image about your organization until you know the real perceptions held by your publics?

The bottom line on research is that it affects the bottom line – whatever your organization's bottom line might be. In the long run it can save you money, time, resources, and effort.

Research can accomplish many things. The following are some of the things it can accomplish for public relations:

1. Determine the type and size of the public relations effort required.
2. Determine the extent to which there is a need for this approach.
3. Provide information to help you determine the precise public relations problem or opportunity facing your organization.
4. Target your specific public(s). (We'll discuss publics more in a later chapter.)
5. Describe the specific characteristics of your public(s).
6. Assist in the articulation of your message(s).
7. Identify appropriate and potentially effective vehicles, tactics, and channels to reach specific publics.
8. Enhance the credibility of the public relations function with top management.

Problem or opportunity?

Being able to recognize a **problem** or **opportunity** and to define it succinctly is one of the most important outcomes of the data analysis in the research phase and no research is complete without it. The following are useful definitions that will help both you and your client/ employer to understand the planning process that will follow.

> A public relations problem is a relationship or communication issue that has been identified as a result of past events, current activities, and future projections, and which is likely to impede the organization from reaching its goals.

Thus a problem emanates directly from weaknesses in the relationships that an organization has with one or more publics. A problem may be a public's lack of **information** about the organization, its policies, its products or services, or issues it represents, for example. It may also be an **attitude** or perception issue: One or more publics may hold negative perceptions about the organization or what it represents. This negative attitude may or may not have resulted (yet) in the public taking action on that attitude. This, of course, leads naturally to the final kind of problem, **actions** that a public has taken as a result of its unhealthy relationship with the organization. When determining an organization's public relations problems, a PR practitioner must consider all of these domains.

An opportunity offers a different perspective.

A public relations opportunity is the identification of a juncture of events and objectives that provides an optimal window for using communication strategies to enhance an organization's internal and/or external relationships and thus further the organization's goals.

An opportunity emerges from an analysis of the organization's strengths in its relationships and communications activities with its publics (what's working well) and its responses to its environment. In addition, strengths may be identified within the organization itself. For example, the appointment of a new CEO with a fundamental understanding of the value of public relations as a management function may present a number of opportunities to strengthen relationships and PR processes within the organization.

How research is done

Research textbooks discuss two major categories of research. First, **academic research** is conducted, usually by scholars, in an effort to add to the general body of knowledge in a particular discipline. The practical applications may not be immediately apparent. For example, a public relations professor might research public relations ethics to explain how and why PR practitioners do what they do. Then he or she might develop a theory to explain the ethical decision-making process.

Applied research, on the other hand, is research that is conducted within a professional field. Both scholars and practitioners might be engaged in applied research, but usually for different reasons. In the process of planning and managing public relations strategies and campaigns, public relations practitioners are engaged in applied research.

In terms of techniques that public relations practitioners might use to gather data during the research phase of developing the PR plan, there are two general categories. **Secondary research** is the term used to describe the process of collecting information from sources where the original data have been accumulated already. Examples of secondary research sources are as follows:

- archival material
- governmental statistical compilations
- trade organization statistics
- library collections
- organizational publications and records
- online data bases

In spite of the monikers "primary" and secondary," secondary research is usually necessary as a first step before primary research can be planned and conducted. Once this secondary source material is collected, the public relations practitioner often needs to conduct **primary research**. In other words, you need to gather firsthand information that is not already available from any other source. The following are examples of primary public relations research methods:

- surveys in general
- readership surveys in particular
- focus groups
- interviews
- observation

If you know anything about typical data gathering in public relations already, you might be wondering where **media monitoring** fits in. The information you are collecting is in a secondary source (mass media), but you are using the information collected in a new and unique way and no other organization is likely to be using the same framework as you are for analyzing the information. Thus, for our purposes in public relations, it is useful to consider media monitoring as part of your primary research that is conducted on an ongoing basis, not just in preparation for the development of a program or campaign plan.

The communication audit

One type of public relations research tool that uses both primary and secondary methods for data-gathering is the **communication audit**. The terms communication audit and **public relations audit** are usually used interchangeably, although some people in the PR field differentiate between them by suggesting that the public relations audit focuses more on the communication climate within and outside the organization, on the quality of the relationships with publics, and on the role of the public relations function itself. We'll define the communication / public relations audit as follows:

> The communication/public relations audit is a research tool that examines and assesses all aspects of an organization's activities, including the internal communication climate, to diagnose the extent to which each public is receiving and responding to the messages targeted toward them and the quality of the relationships engendered by the organization through its communication and activities.

Whenever a public relations practitioner is faced with a new employer, client, or industry, it is almost impossible not to do one, at least to answer the question: Where are we now?

The data collection carried out in the research phase of the public relations planning process almost always requires a combination of techniques. Thus, before you plunge into the archives or the creation of a survey instrument (see recommended resources for further details), you need to create a plan of how you are going to research what aspects of the organization and its publics, and why.

Characterizing relationships with publics

One of the "ends" of the research phase is the ability to assess the quality of the relationships that the organization has developed with its publics as a result of proactive and reactive communication and organizational activities. This assessment of the quality of relationships is the first stage of the data analysis.

The answers to the following questions will help the public relations practitioner to characterize the relationships that the organization has with specific publics so that these may be created, maintained, or improved as a result of the subsequent plan.

- What degree of credibility does the organization have in the eyes of this public?
- To what extent does this public understand (a) our mission; (b) our values; (c) our policies?
- To what extent do members of this public believe that they benefit from a relationship with this organization?
- How much conflict has the organization faced with this public recently? Farther in the past?
- How much conflict is the organization likely to face with this public in the future?
- How does this public act toward this organization and what do these actions say about the relationship? (See chapter 3 resource by Grunig & Hon 1999 for further information).

Data that relate to the answers to these questions will be key in ensuring a complete analysis – a crucial part of the research process.

Analyzing the information

Unlike the process of **synthesis**, which takes parts of something and forms them into a logical whole, the process of **analysis** takes the whole of something and breaks it down into its parts. The report about that process is also referred to as an analysis (thus, the term analysis is used as a part of the plan you will write).

The analysis is a significant part of the research phase. Without this process, all you have is a body of information that is both unwieldy and useless. You have to do something with it!

It is often said that individuals either possess an analytical mind or they do not. Learning the skills necessary to analyze data is, however, quite possible. In the practice of public relations, the ability to analyze data and to determine an organization's strengths, weaknesses, problems and opportunities comes as a result of not only individual talent, but also from experience and judgment. Any good public relations practitioner can develop this talent, and it is a key element of learning to think like a manager.

As you gather data about the organization and its public relations and communication activities, you need to have a way of putting that data into categories and determining the relationships among pieces of data.

If you have survey results, you might use statistics as part of your analytical process (e.g. averages, standard deviations, chi squares). If you have a series of organizational print materials, you might use the process of content analysis. Content analysis can be very informal, or can be a very formalized process of identification and analysis of specific pieces of content. Analyzing print materials might also use the application of any number of available readability indices to determine reading level.

One aspect of analysis that is key to figuring out what to do next is to be able to answer the following questions:

- What aspects of the organization's external environment are currently affecting it either positively or negatively?

- What aspects of the organization's external environment are likely to affect it in the future?

- How would you describe the organization's internal environment?

- Who are the organization's publics?

- Has the organization accurately identified and described its publics, both current and future?

- How can these publics be categorized?

- How would you characterize the organization's short and long-term relationships with each public?

- What messages does the organization convey to each public?

- Are these the messages that the organization intends to convey?

- What vehicles and channels are used to convey these messages to each public?

- How effectively do these vehicles convey the intended messages?

- To what extent do they convey unintended messages? How do they do this (overtly and subliminally)?

- What organizational actions convey intended and unintended messages to specific publics?

- What are the organization's public relations strengths and weaknesses?

- What are the public relations problems?

- What are the public relations opportunities?

The narrative report that discusses all of these questions constitutes what will become the **situational analysis** in the public relations plan. It is important to note that if you are working on a plan that is designed to target one or more specific publics, the foregoing questions need to focus on that aspect of the organization and its environment. For example, if you are developing an internal communications plan, your main focus is on employees and other internal publics (such as volunteers), and only on other publics and the external environment to the extent that these affect your target public.

Using a table as a working tool when you are analyzing the data can be useful. It might look something like the following.

Figure 2.1
Data Table

Public	Message(s)	Vehicles	Assessment

Here is what you should do with each of the columns in this table:

Public: This column is the place where you identify the current publics recognized by the organization. Some of these might include media, the community, employees, volunteers, Board of Directors, governmental agencies, members and so on. But each is dealt with separately.

Message(s): This column enables you to identify the messages that are *currently* being transmitted to the specific publics you have identified. This includes both intended and unintended messages transmitted by either communication or other activities of the organization. Often the messages that the public actually receives and interprets are not the same as those intended by the organization. You need to know this. In addition, it might be time for the intended message to change.

Vehicles: This is where you delineate the communication vehicles that are currently being used to disseminate messages or create the organization's image and reputation. Again, these are categorized according to the specific public identified, but remember that organizations use some of their vehicles to reach multiple audiences. Even the process of writing newsletter, for example, under a series of publics, might suggest that the organization is trying to accomplish too much with one piece. On the other hand, it may become apparent that one vehicle is not being fully utilized.

Assessment: This column is probably the most important part of this data table. This is where the analysis really begins. In the assessment column, you make an initial evaluation of the success or failure of the public/message/vehicle and you begin to discover strengths and weaknesses in the public relations activities of the organization. Here are some questions that you might consider in this column: Does the message that is being transmitted seem appropriate? Is the message an intended one? Is any message being transmitted? Does the vehicle targeted at a particular public seem appropriate? What is the level of the quality? Is there consistency of messages? Are there any other publics with which the organization ought to have relationships? Is this tool being evaluated at all?

There are two important considerations in using this kind of a tool for data collection and analysis at this stage. First, it is a reflection of the current situation *not the situation that you intend to exist after the implementation of a strategic plan.* Second, it provides you with only a *superficial examination* of the situation at this stage and is not complete enough to examine elaborate two-way communication efforts on the organization's part. This table is useful to you both as you collect data – it can allow you to formulate a visual picture of where you are and what are the relationships among the variables – and it can also serve later as a way to present the data. The table becomes a companion to the narrative portion of the analysis.

Another key aspect of the data analysis is determining the organization's strengths and weaknesses in their communication and relationships with their publics. Finally, from these strengths and weaknesses, the public relations strategist must determine the organization's problems and opportunities (refer back to our definitions and descriptions earlier in the chapter).

Writing up your analysis is the final step. You might consider using the questions posed earlier as a guideline for that written narrative analysis. Once you have your data analyzed, you are ready to move on to the development of your plan.

The following pages provide you with work sheets that you might find helpful in organizing both your data and your written analysis.

The first is a **Data Table** as we discussed earlier. Use it as you collect your data to identify the publics with whom the organization has relationships, the messages actually communicated and the vehicles and activities used to communicate those messages. In addition, it provides you the first opportunity to organize your initial assessment of the state of the communication/public relations activities of the organization.

After you have completed the table this far, examine the data again to figure out if there are other publics with whom the organization ought to be developing relationships but is not, and add these to the table. This way of organizing the information will allow you to proceed with the narrative analysis and the determination of strengths and weaknesses.

This leads us to the **Problem & Opportunity Analysis** worksheet. Begin with a listing of public relations-related strengths and weaknesses in the left-hand column. On the right-hand side, consider corresponding problems and opportunities. This final assessment of problems and opportunities is translated into a narrative description of how you came to determine each one.

The final worksheet for this chapter is the **Data Analysis Check List**. Use it initially to determine if you have collected all necessary data. Then, when you have completed your written analysis, use it as a checklist to evaluate the completeness of your narrative report.

Data Table

Audit results of current activities / relationships

Public	Message(s)	Vehicles	Assessment

Problem / Opportunity Analysis

PR Strengths	Potential Opportunities

PR Weaknesses	Potential Problems

Data Analysis Checklist

As you prepare to translate your data analysis into a narrative situational analysis, use the following checklist to ensure that you have collected all relevant information and analyzed it in terms of its relationship to the organization's public relations goals.

The analysis contains the following:

- ❑   key aspects of the organization's external environment

- ❑   current and future effects of key elements of external environment

- ❑   key aspects of the organization's internal environment

- ❑   current and future effects of key elements of internal environment

- ❑   identification of publics

- ❑   description of publics

- ❑   consequences of publics for organization and vice versa

- ❑   description of organization's relationships with publics

- ❑   identification of current messages to each public

- ❑   comparison of actual with intended messages

- ❑   identification of vehicles used to convey messages to each public

- ❑   effectiveness of each vehicle in conveying intended messages

- ❑   description of any unintentional messages

- ❑   identification of public relations strengths and weaknesses

- ❑   identification of key public relations problem and/or opportunity

- ❑   extent to which the organization has adapted to environmental pressures/publics

Chapter 3

The Planning Phase

Vocabulary

- 📁 communication framework
- 📁 communication strategy
- 📁 goals & objectives
- 📁 public
- 📁 message
- 📁 communication vehicles

The Planning Phase

The Plan

Once the data collection and analysis of the research phase are essentially complete, you have enough information to get you started on the development of a concrete plan to tackle the identified problem(s) and/or opportunity(ies). Keep in mind, however, that although we tend to talk about the four phases of the process as if they were discrete and as if the process itself were linear, in fact it is neither. Collecting and analyzing data may be necessary throughout the process whenever new information becomes available. This ongoing process enables you to make corrections as you go along.

There are four key elements to the planning phase. These four elements are as follows:

- defining and describing publics
- constructing the objectives
- articulating the messages
- choosing the medium(a) and tools/ vehicles

Before we examine each of these more closely, however, we need to describe exactly what it is we will have at the end of this part of the process. What are these four elements going to describe when they come together at the end?

One of the ways you might present this at the end of the process is by the use of a **communication/public relations plan framework**. Like an outline of a more detailed report, this framework sets the groundwork for a more comprehensive strategy. It is a brief glimpse of an organization, its publics, PR objectives, intended messages, vehicles and approaches, and an overview of how the plan will be evaluated. Every public relations practitioner needs to know how to write such a framework.

Public relations managers also need to be confident in their abilities to put all of this together as a **communication/public relations strategy**. This presents the thoroughly researched, comprehensive plan that delineates clearly the analysis, the problem / opportunity, objectives and communication activities, and evaluation strategies. It involves a detailed analysis of what the organization's relationships are today, where it wants them to be (in 3 months, 1 year, 5 years, for example), and how it will get there. This document is actually written during the planning phase, but considers research, planning, implementation, and evaluation.

Defining publics

During the research phase, the public relations practitioner examines the place of the organization within its social, political, and economic environment. At the same time, the publics that have consequences for the organization and for whom the organization has consequences emerge. These publics are obviously groups of people, but for purposes of planning for the public relations needs of organizations, you are going to need a more specific definition.

Over the years, many public relations authors and practitioners have defined publics (refer to any of the general resources listed for chapter 1 to see examples of these definitions). In practice, we often hear publics defined as groups of people who have a shared interest and are aware of that commonality. On the other hand, it can be argued that members of a public identified by the organization may not be aware of their shared interest or the characteristic they have in common. Other approaches to defining publics could consider geography, socioeconomic status, gender, race, ethnicity, religion, and any other demographic or psychographic factors.

All of these ways of defining publics are useful to public relations practitioners in specific circumstances, but they each have their limitations in practice. Here is a working definition that is useful

> A public is a group of people who share a common interest, demographic, or psychographic characteristic, as defined by the public relations function of the organization, and whose actions are either influenced by or have an influence on the organization.

When examining this definition, keep in mind that publics can form on their own in response to organizational activities, policies, or products to pressure the organization. Unless, however, they are eventually identified in the public relations process, they cannot be considered in the strategy. Failing to identify them – either by design or inadvertently – can have major negative consequences for the organization. For example, when creating a 5-year strategic public relations plan, you might define your "community" by drawing geographic boundaries: your neighborhood, your city, your region, your entire country even might be the community within which you function and with which you must develop a relationship. On the other hand, an activist group might define itself in response to your organization. They have created the boundaries, but when developing your PR plan, you, too must define them.

Publics can be internal or external. Their activities may currently be influencing the organization or that influence may not yet be felt. They may be ranked in order of priority to the organization (and this is likely to change). If you're dealing with controversy, they may be categorized as for, against, or neutral. It is often useful to use the systems diagram that we discussed in chapter 1 to plot out the publics and view their relationships with the organization.

The following is a generic list of some of the most commonly described publics:

- employees
- volunteers (in nonprofits)
- members (in memberships organizations)
- financial donors (usually in nonprofits)
- investors (in publicly held corporations)
- media (mass and industry-specific)
- community
- government (various levels)
- regulatory bodies
- consumers/clients (of goods and/or services)

An astute public relations practitioner will be constantly aware of other potential groupings of people that might constitute an important public to the organization at present or in the future. For example, a pharmaceutical company that uses animals in drug research must be constantly aware of animal rights activists in their community. And if there isn't such a group at present, like-minded people could come together for the purpose of targeting the organization. The data collected in the research phase about current publics and the organization's environment provide clues about who the important publics are or should be.

Constructing objectives

An ability to construct clear, useful objectives is perhaps the essential key to being an effective planner. You need to know exactly what you intend to accomplish through these activities that will follow.

Although there are many definitions of goals and objectives, let's think of a goal as a broad, but pointed statement of what this plan is intended to accomplish. Objectives are the specific outcomes sought for each public being considered in the plan.

> Outcome objectives are specific statements of destination that assist in the accomplishment of the stated overall goal. They are clear, measurable, realistic, and include a time frame.

Clear objectives are stated succinctly, employing language that can be understood by all those who will be involved in the achievement of the outcomes. There can be no argument about their meaning. **Measurable objectives** are stated in such a way that the outcome identified can be quantified in some way. This is not always easy but must be attempted. Measurable objectives answer the question: How much of an effect are we seeking? This will eventually allow the PR practitioner to determine the degree of intended effect and to identify those unintended effects that might have resulted from the actions taken. **Realistic objectives** recognize that there are limitations to what can reasonably be accomplished given the organization's resources, environmental situations, and time frames. Finally, objectives with a **time frame** indicate when the outcome is to be expected: They limit the time for implementation of a plan after which time the approach should be evaluated against the objective itself.

The best way to illustrate outcome objectives is to examine a situation. Consider the case of a not-for-profit membership organization that has been experiencing a downward trend in its membership over the past four years. The research indicates that the external image of the organization is dated and unprofessional, and this is contributing to loss of members and inability to attract new ones. It seems clear, then, that the objectives of the public relations strategy might be to improve the organization's image in the eyes of specific external publics (potential members), and perhaps even with internal publics (current members). That's a useful overall goal that is likely to shore up many aspects of the organization's relationships, but it isn't an outcome objective that meets our criteria. It isn't specific enough and it isn't measurable. Here are two outcome objectives that would contribute to meeting the overall goal of improving or changing the organization's image:

- To increase membership by 30% over the next 8 months.

- To retain current members and have them articulate satisfaction with the organization by the end of the year.

The first objective is clear, concise, measurable, and understandable and it includes a time frame for completion. The second one is as well, but it addresses an issue that you will often face. Exactly how do you measure some more nebulous public relations effects such as satisfaction, positive attitude, or image? This objective holds a clue. It indicates that you will measure not satisfaction itself, but articulation of that satisfaction. This kind of objective is useful in another way, too. In it lurks a clue about the kind of tactic or tool you will need to develop. In this case, you will need to devise an opportunity for the current members to speak about this issue. Sometimes the outcome is more qualitative than quantitative and you have to deal with this in as specific a manner as possible.

What is wrong with the following objective?

■ To improve the organization's external image by 30%.

Not only is this vague (exactly what does an image consist of?), but it is clearly not rational to consider placing a quantitative value on image. In itself, it isn't measurable. Here is a better way of stating the kind of outcome you might be seeking.

■ To enhance the organization's image in the community as evidenced by a 50% increase in positive reporting about organizational community initiatives in the community newspaper.

Obviously, this objective presupposes that you have counted both the amount and direction (positive or negative) of past coverage of events in this medium.

Relationship objectives

Public relations is in the business of developing and maintaining relationships with important publics, thus it is necessary to consider not only the communication outcomes but also the relationship outcomes.

Communication outcomes are often framed in terms of knowledge, attitudes, and behaviors that are desirable from a public relations perspective. Obviously, these are important in the development and nurturing of relationships, but recently, public relations has become more interested on the actual quality of the relationships themselves. Modern PR must, as much as possible, try to focus on the kind of relationship that the organization wants and needs to have with its various publics. But how can you develop measurable objectives for something as seemingly nebulous as a relationship?

Although there are no hard and fast rules or even guidelines about this, there are some aspects of relationships that are useful to the public relations effort of the organization. You might consider some of the following questions when formulating these objectives:

■ To what extent is it important that this public trust the organization?
■ To what extent is it important that this public feel positively about this organization?
■ To what extent is it important that this public feel that this organization gives as much as it takes from this public? (See the Institute for Public Relations monograph by Grunig & Hon listed among the resources.)

Clearly, there are many issues to consider when trying to determine the kind of relationship your organization would like to develop and maintain with publics. These questions will help you to begin to consider relationship outcomes and to include such objectives when developing a public relations plan. If you need further in-depth information on this topic, you can refer to the resource list later in the workbook.

Considering processes

Often when you are developing objectives, it is easy to forget that what they really are is an answer to the question: Where do we want to go? Instead, you might fall into the trap of considering only processes. These processes are not ends in themselves, rather, they help to guide the selection and development of communication vehicles. For example, the following objectives are more accurately described as **process objectives** than as **outcome objectives**:

- ■ To communicate regularly with members.
- ■ To ensure timeliness in all communication.
- ■ To enhance opportunities for two-way communication.

Although each of these is admirable and may even be a necessary part of the objectives of the public relations department in your organization, they are not really strategic. They only speak to the actual process of conducting the public relations and communication activities. Indeed, they are focused more on the PR function rather than on the public. They are very useful objectives if one of the problems you have is the quality of the public relations effort itself. If that is the first PR problem that you identify, then these objectives may be useful as a first step toward the focus you will eventually develop on publics.

Keying objectives to publics

The final issue related to objectives is to consider the intended target of each one. The strongest communication plans key the objectives toward specific publics. For example, in considering media relations, the objectives would be directed specifically toward the media. These objectives about what the public relations planning process aims to achieve are related to what the organization aims to achieve in community relations, employee relations, investor relations, relations with activist organizations, and so on.

Keying objectives to specific publics enables a more directed selection of communication strategies later. Although you might select a particular strategy or vehicle that can achieve more than one objectives and is directed toward more than one public, you will eventually need to examine the outcomes for each public separately.

Developing messages

Public relations focuses on managing communications between an organization and its publics for the purpose of developing and maintaining long-term, mutually beneficial relationships with those publics. The heart of the PR activity is the message or messages that the organization conveys to its publics in both word and deed. And make no mistake about it, even if the organization does not consciously consider the messages it sends out or develop them purposefully, publics, both external and internal, will see and hear messages all the same and will respond to the organization based on their perception of the messages.

Organizational actions often speak louder than words. It is the responsibility of the public relations function of any organization to ensure that all messages conveyed to various publics are, indeed, the messages that are intended. This naturally presupposes that you've given active consideration to what you really intend to say and that the communication vehicles chosen to convey those messages do so accurately and to the intended public. Thus, at this point in the planning process, once the publics have been identified and the specific objectives for this plan have been set out, the next step is to develop core messages.

> A core message is a succinct statement of the core information that the organization intends to convey to its publics with the intended tone.

Once you have considered the actual core message that you intend to convey via both words and actions, it needs to be considered in the development of every public relations activity that you will develop in an effort to achieve your objectives. Remember, the message has both overt and subliminal aspects and both are important in the eventual perceptions that arise as a result.

Choosing public relations vehicles

The final aspect of the planning phase is selecting appropriate public relations vehicles – the channels and tools that you have reason to believe will successfully convey the intended messages and develop the intended relationships with your publics. The information that you have about your publics – for example, their preferred channels for receiving messages, their level of interest in your organization and its mission, their level of understanding of the issues, their demographics – will help greatly in selecting channels that are most likely to achieve your objectives.

For example, selecting direct mail to disseminate your community relations message is probably not going to be as effective as if you involve your organization in a current community activity or develop a new community activity. Then your actions and the specific communications surrounding those actions will disseminate the message and nurture the relationship.

Here are some things to keep in mind when selecting channels and tools or vehicles:

- This is a creative process. Begin with brainstorming and be open to new ways of looking at old things.
- The tools must be keyed to specific objectives (although one tool might be used to achieve more than one objective, or several tools might be needed to achieve a single objective).
- The channel or tool must be considered in relation to the specific target public.
- There must be a rationale for selecting both the channel and the tool or vehicle.

Consider first the creative aspect of designing and selecting channels and vehicles. This means that you need to stop thinking in a linear fashion about communication/public relations tools and tactics. A kind of initial brainstorming process allows you to move away from the more familiar strategies to the more creative – perhaps simply a new way of approaching an old strategy. For example, developing a new newsletter may not be the best way to enhance morale among employees. You might consider developing an award that recognizes employees' volunteer activities. The process of nominating and selecting is all part of the communication activity and then the publication of the identity of the winner can even become part of your community relations program.

Also, your first inclination to use mass media (a channel) might be to look for a news angle and disseminate a news release (a tool/vehicle). Even if mass media appear to be the channel of choice in the situation under consideration, there are other tools that you might consider: querying an editor of a feature-type magazine, a newspaper feature, a television interview on a news magazine show, or even paid advertising. Creativity in planning requires that you go beyond your first – and often over-used – inclination.

Communication vehicles that are not keyed to specific objectives run the risk of wasting time, money, and effort. Why would you implement a communication activity that wasn't strategically designed to achieve a specific objective? This is tied in with the issue of rationale. What makes you believe that this approach you are proposing is likely to work with this particular public? Part of your rationale relates to the outcome you're trying to achieve. Can this combination of channel and vehicle actually accomplish what you really

Rationales for channels and strategies

want? Do you have any external basis or past experience on which to base this decision?

You need a strong basis in communication and audience analysis theories and you need to keep up with what is going on in the field. The inherent empirical nature of public relations – in other words, it relies largely on the extent to which we have experience with a particular approach rather than on some scholar's theory of what should work – means that you can learn a lot from case studies presented in both the academic and the popular literature of the industry. You need to keep current. The development of rationales also provides you with a basis on which you can lean when you're trying to convince employers and/or clients that what you are proposing actually has some chance of working.

Using the worksheets

There are three worksheets accompanying this chapter.

The first is **Identification & Categorization of Publics**, which is designed to help you to identify the publics that you will be focusing on for this particular plan. The decision about these publics will be drawn from your research data – considering both the current publics with whom the organization has relationships as well as those with whom it should. Sometimes, you may have only one public if this is a small plan designed to accomplish a very specific, time-limited goal. The systems-like chart will give you a visual representation of the relationship between the organization and its relevant publics as well as a chance to consider environmental pressures and the type of communication.

The second worksheet is a **Checklist for Outcome Objectives**. Especially when you first begin to develop objectives, it's useful to have such a checklist to evaluate their quality before you move on.

The third worksheet pulls all your previous work together as a **Public Relations Plan** worksheet. It puts together in chart form the plan that you are creating. It keys messages to publics, to objectives, to channels and tactics, to the accomplishment of specific objectives. Use this as a first step in determining strategic approaches and to visualize the connections between objectives, publics, and approaches to make the best use of each.

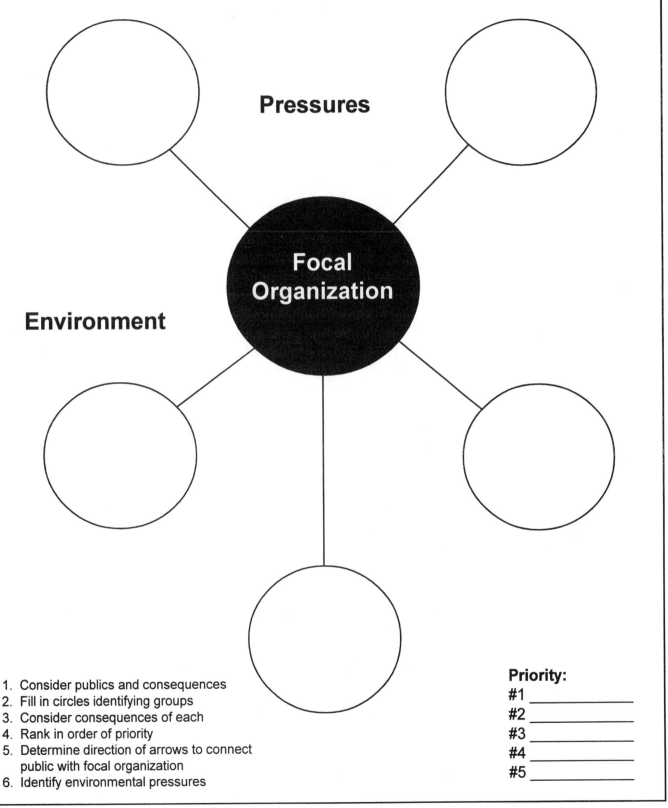

Identification & Categorization of Publics

Pressures

Focal Organization

Environment

1. Consider publics and consequences
2. Fill in circles identifying groups
3. Consider consequences of each
4. Rank in order of priority
5. Determine direction of arrows to connect public with focal organization
6. Identify environmental pressures

Priority:

#1 _____
#2 _____
#3 _____
#4 _____
#5 _____

Checklist for Development of Objectives

Once you have developed your outcome objectives for each public, use this checklist to determine the quality of each objective. Rewrite any objective that doesn't measure up.

❑   The wording is clear and concise.

❑   The members of this organization will understand this objective.

❑   The stated outcome is realistic.

❑   The stated outcome is feasible for this organization, at this time.

❑   There is an explicit date for completion.

❑   The stated outcome is measurable.

❑   The stated outcome is a communication/public relations effect.

Public Relations Plan Worksheet

Overall Message

Public #1

Message

PR Objectives:
1.
2.
3.

Tools & Strategies:

Public #2

Message

PR Objectives:
1.
2.
3.

Tools & Strategies:

Public #3

Message

PR Objectives:
1.
2.
3.

Tools & Strategies:

Public #4

Message

PR Objectives:
1.
2.
3.

Tools & Strategies:

Chapter 4

Managing Implementation

Vocabulary

- ☐ control
- ☐ influence
- ☐ management
- ☐ leadership
- ☐ delegation
- ☐ budget
- ☐ Gantt chart
- ☐ flow sheets

Revisiting management definitions

Implementation of the public relations plan is the third step of the public relations process. It implies carrying out the activities developed in the planning step. For the public relations technician, that's all there is to know. From a technical perspective, it is now time to get to work on carrying out the technical aspects of the plan. But for the public relations manager, a crucial part of the management process is just beginning.

We began our attempt to define management in chapter 1. We discussed the fact that there are as many definitions of management as there are people writing about the subject. Now as we move into the practical application of the concept, the following commonalities of the definitions emerge as key to our understanding.

- 🗀 **Management is a process.**

- 🗀 **Management involves and concentrates on reaching the organization's goals.**

- 🗀 **Management involves working with and through people.**

- 🗀 **Management involves working with and through organizational resources.**

We can see from these aspects of management that, in general, managers are concerned with managing people, financial resources, time, and quality.

The first aspect of this definition means that management is not a "thing" and it is not static. It continually changes because it involves a series of continuing and related activities. Management is clearly not something that you do once in a while.

Next, management of the organization focuses on reaching **organizational goals**. For the public relations function, this means ensuring that any public relations strategies developed are in line with the overall goals of the organization. The communication and public relations activities are not ends in themselves, rather, they contribute to the organization's bottom line.

Managers must have highly evolved "people" skills. If managing the public relations process means managing the activities of people, it means that the manager needs to be able to develop good rapport, assess the strengths and weakness of the staff, **delegate** appropriate activities to appropriate staff members, assess the work accomplished, and enhance the working environment by creating a climate of cooperation and collaboration.

Managers also need knowledge and skills in organizing other resources of the organization. These include, primarily, time, money, and quality. Tools that managers use to manage these resources include **budgets, flow sheets,** and **time and activity management charts.**

The historical context

Historically, there have been many disagreements about how best to analyze and react to management situations. Early in the 20th century, many of those studying management as a discipline were focused on the actual activities that the workers performed. Most management theorists focused on the one best way to carry out a job, whether it was shoveling coal or laying bricks. These "management consultants" were quite successful in helping organizations of various sorts to decrease the number of people required to do this physical labor and to increase their profit margins. There was little concern, however, about the people aspect of the job.

Other consultants examined this classical approach to management and decided that the human factor needed more consideration. These theorists injected such elements as employee morale and motivation into the management systems and came up with ways that organizations could adapt themselves to their people. Such work paved the way for systems of reward to be used to enhance the work an individual was prepared to perform for an employer.

Other approaches to management include the more recent management science approach, which borrows from mathematical and scientific techniques that include observation, deduction and testing, and the development of ways of dealing with contingencies. One approach to management theory that we have already examined is the systems approach. As this approach involves examining relationships, it is a very useful framework for applying to the management of public relations (see chapter 1).

Management and leadership

Before we move on to specific aspects of how to manage the implementation of a project, we need to examine the relationship between management as a general concept, and the concept of leadership. To the casual observer, they may appear to be one and the same – but in fact they are quite different in both focus and skills required.

> Management ensures the day-to-day accomplishment of organizational activities designed to move the organization in the direction of its ultimate goal. Leadership, on the other hand, is the force that determines that direction and ultimate goal.

Leaders are those visionaries who can visualize the future and where the organization should be heading. Great leaders can communicate that vision to their followers and gain their support and "buy-in." The managers may set the more short-term goals that lead toward the vision, and are able to communicate those goals to co-workers, gaining their support and buy-in for the approach to achieving those short-term goals.

In any discussion of leadership and management the question always arises of whether managers are leaders and whether leaders need to be managers. There is no universal answer to these questions, but logic leads us to conclude that managers need not be leaders in the visionary sense (although it wouldn't hurt), but need to be able to lead people in day-to-day activities. Any group of people working together needs working leadership to assign tasks, arbitrate in conflicts, and evaluate activities. The manager in this position also provides the communication link between the workers and the leadership of the organization.

On the other hand, a great leader may not be a great manager. This leader may be completely versed in the issues and trends in the organization's external environment, exhibiting all the hallmarks of a true futurist, but be relatively inept at the day-to-day activities required to manage a project. Would it be useful for a leader to be a good manager? Of course it would be helpful if this individual had experience in more junior management positions in an organization, if for no other reason than to enhance his or her credibility in the eyes of the followers. But when leaders regularly involve themselves in those day-to-day management activities, it can cause problems both for the managers whose jobs they are intruding on and for the long-term vision of the organization. It's difficult, if not impossible, for a great leader to be future-focused when enmeshed in the daily grind of managing projects.

Budgets as management tools

Let's begin our discussion of management tools with an examination of budgeting, as this is likely the first step you will need to take in managing the implementation of the public relations plan. More than any other aspect of managing projects, budgeting seems to frighten public relations practitioners. In reality, though, if you're like the rest of us you've probably been acquiring experience with budgeting since you were very young.

If your parents provided you with an allowance, you soon recognized that it would only go so far. If you wanted to buy something special with your allowance and you didn't have enough money, you had to make a decision. Either you would wait until you did have enough money, or you allocated your available resources in a different way. Perhaps you settled for a less expensive item, or even two less expensive items. In any case, you already know something about allocating financial resources.

As you got older, your expenses likely grew, but then so did your income. Thus, even if you believe yourself to be hopeless in sticking to a personal budget, you've probably had occasion to examine your income on the one hand versus your expenses on the other. This encompasses the basic concepts of budgeting.

> A budget for a public relations project is a financial plan for allocating specific sums of money to specific activities required for the achievement of the objectives.

Thus a budget performs two main functions: It is a control mechanism for the activities necessary to achieve the objectives, and it is a communication tool to explain public relations activities and objectives to non-PR managers and other organizational leaders.

In public relations, there are two general categories of budgets that we deal with. The first is a **program budget** or **project budget**. It is a more global way to think about the allocation of financial resources in the public relations activities of an organization. It refers to a specific sum of money that is allocated to cover a program or project, and considers the public relations activities in a holistic way. This contrasts with a **line item budget** where the public relations function is budgeted by allowing the department specific sums for items such as printing, design services, postage, couriers, office supplies, and so on. This is a more piecemeal way to budget for public relations activities. If, however, your departmental budget *is* a line item budget, you have no alternative in project budgeting but to use those same items and budget them into the project in that way. This approach sometimes makes it more difficult to include new items that may not be in the departmental item list and to reallocate budgeted proportions for specific items.

When faced with a program budget for public relations activities, the general approach to budgeting the specific project is to assign a sum of money as a project budget. That sum is then broken down to cover the activities that are required by the plan you have already developed. It should be clear at this point that considerations about budgets should also be made during the planning phase so that you are not now faced with champagne activities planned on a beer budget, as the saying goes.

The project manager then takes the public relations plan already developed and breaks it down into specific activities and items that need to be covered in order to achieve the objectives. Here are some of the things that you need to consider in the initial development of a realistic, accurate budget.

- Who will be involved in the implementation?
- What tasks will each person be assigned to complete?
- Realistically, how long will it take each person to complete his or her tasks?
- What materials will be required?
- What outside services will be required (e.g., printers, couriers, postage, models, actors, studio time, clipping services, photographers, audio-visual services, room rentals, equipment rentals)?
- Do you have estimates of costs from all required outside services?

Once all of these are taken into consideration, you'll need to compare the grand total to the budgeted amount and revise as necessary. It takes professional judgment to consider where money can be saved and where it needs to be maintained to still be able to accomplish the objectives. Sometimes it is necessary to rethink some aspects of the objectives (are they still realistic given the resources available?), or the communication vehicles selected (is there another effective vehicle that we can use and still stay within budget?).

The manager is also responsible for determining at which points it will be feasible to reexamine the budget, in process, to ensure that the project is still on target. This allows the budget to become another control tool.

Deadlines and time management

Managing time means managing *people's* time. It means being able to schedule activities so that the project comes in not only on budget, as we discussed previously, but **on deadline**. Public relations practitioners are well aware that the ability to meet deadlines is crucial to the successful practice of PR. As such, individual public relations practitioners may be fully aware of how long it takes them to carry out specific tasks and thus meet those deadlines. The public relations manager, on the other hand, must estimate how long it will take any number of people to carry out any number of tasks, and create a schedule that considers both people and project requirements. An important project requirement is the prerequisite nature of some of those activities. In other words, some activities must be completed, or at least in progress, before others can be started. The manager needs to juggle all of these.

Public relations managers use a variety of tools to schedule time. The simplest is the one that many people use for personal time management – the to-do list. These laundry lists of activities are useful but have serious limitations. They don't consider priorities, how long each task will take, or if any are prerequisites to others. Thus, as a management tool they are only the first step toward controlling deadlines. What you really need is some kind of action plan that organizes those activities.

The **Gantt chart** is one tool that managers in general have been using since early in the 20th century when management consultant Henry Gantt developed it. In simple terms, a Gantt chart takes that laundry list of activities and places them on a chart that has activities down one side and time lapse across. It then uses bars to plot out the time it will take to complete each individual task, considering when the activity should be started and how it may overlap other activities. The chart is a plan for time management and just as a budget can be used during the course of the project to determine the extent to which you are likely to stay on budget, the Gantt chart can be used to determine whether or not you are likely to meet your deadline. One of the most important aspects of the Gantt chart, however, is that it isn't carved in stone. If it looks like the plan will not allow you to bring the project to a conclusion on time, then the schedule must be changed and you need to update your chart.

Figure 4.1 illustrates what a simple Gantt chart might look like.

Figure 4.1
Simple Gantt Chart

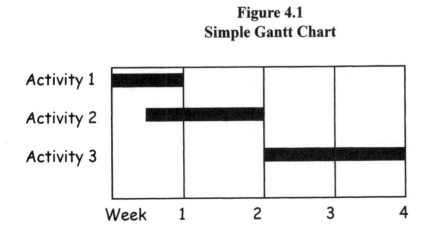

This generic example shows that activity #1 begins at the beginning of week 1 and will be finished by the beginning of week 2. The beginning of activity #2 overlaps with activity #1 and is complete by the end of week 2. This completion is necessary before activity #3 can begin. Activity #3 should be complete by the end of the 4-week project.

As you probably already have figured out, the ability to prepare an accurate and useful Gantt chart, or any other tool for managing time, presupposes that you have the ability to estimate how much time it will take to complete any given task. This is when a manager's previous experience as a public relations technician is extremely useful. If, however, you have never actually carried out the task you are assigning to someone else, you'll need to consult with someone who does have this experience. It is foolhardy to estimate the time required based on nothing more than your gut feeling.

In addition to this professional experience and judgment, there are actually mathematical models for estimating time. To use these, however, requires that you have a sense of both the most optimistic (but realistic) time projection as well as the most pessimistic (but realistic) time projection. The math involves calculating just where that most likely time is: It falls somewhere between the most pessimistic and the most optimistic.

Controlling quality along the way

Now that we have examined the overall concept of management, and have considered the planning management of both time and financial resources, another parameter we need to consider is the management of quality as the project progresses.

There's a lot of talk today about quality assurance, quality control, total quality management, to mention a few of the buzz words. Overall, unlike in the days of the so-called Robber Barons of the early 20th century when big business cared only for its own estimate of its quality, most organizations today are committed to the concept of comprehensive, consumer-focused programs of **quality management**. This is embodied in the notion of TQM (total quality management), which provides an organization with a competitive edge. Managing the quality of a specific public relations project, then, is part of the organization's overall commitment to quality. As the manager of the public relations project, it's your responsibility to find a way to monitor and control the quality.

The first step happens during the planning process. As you select and develop the outcome objectives for the project, you are actually saying that this is the level of outcome you'll achieve. During the final or evaluation phase of the project, you'll figure out if you've met those objectives. At that point you'll be able to say that you did or did not achieve the kind of quality outcome you were planning on. As the project progresses, however, you do need to be aware of the level of quality of the work and the interim outcomes to avoid any surprises at the end.

Some of the parameters that you might consider as on-going measures of quality of the public relations output are:

- consistency
- reliability
- accuracy
- congruence
- honesty

Let's examine each of these parameters to determine the extent to which they might be useful for you to build into your quality monitoring plan. Keep in mind that they are specific to the public relations effort of the organization. If you were monitoring the quality of a manufacturing effort, the quality measures would be different.

Consistency: One of the most important aspects of any organization's messages to its publics is that they be consistent. These messages are carried in both the organization's actions as well as its overt messages. For example, there is both a conscious and a subliminal message carried in the corporate identity program. Are these messages consistent? Are these aspects of this particular project consistent with the organizational norm as well as with one another? Has the creative impulse led you astray? Do all aspects of this particular project carry a consistent style and message?

Reliability: This refers to the ability of the organization's public relations thrust to do what it says it will do. In general, this would refer to the PR department's ability to achieve its overall objectives. In the case of the specific public relations project, do the activities continue to move the project toward successful completion of the objectives set? Are these the kinds of activities that will actually assist the department in achieving its overall goals?

Accuracy: This is an extremely important aspect of quality of the public relations output of any organization. Are all aspects of this project accurate? Is the information in the brochure accurate? Does the photo selected for the media kit accurately display the message intended? Has someone checked all the statistics mentioned in the news release? A public relations project can succeed or fail on the accuracy of the information presented. There is nothing worse than finding an error in a brochure after 2,000 have already been printed, or worse, a member of an external public finding it.

Congruence: This refers to the extent to which all of the aspects of the program "fit" together. Are the parts harmonious? Do they agree with one another? The estimate of ongoing congruence may be based on such concrete aspects as the design parameters (having only one designer can help with this), or on such esoteric things as your overall professional judgment.

Honesty: Clearly, honesty is a value that is held in high esteem in communications professions such as public relations. As a final ongoing check of the quality of a public relations effort, you need to determine the extent to which the project is projecting the messages honestly, and in a way that does not result in misleading the public.

These are overall quality parameters in public relations. For individual aspects of programs you may be able to develop more specific ones. This is merely a starting point.

People: Working with and through

As we began our discussion of management, we defined it partially as working with and through people. The final aspect of managing the public relations project is managing the people involved. Sometimes, you are the only person involved. Other times, the other people with whom you will work during the course of a project are outside designers, printers and others. But frequently, you will have one or more other public relations people working with you on this project. As the manager of the project, you are responsible for getting the most out of those people while assisting them to maintain their morale and motivation.

Delegation is one of the most important and most frequently discussed people skills in managing projects.

> Delegation is entrusting another individual with the authority to make decisions about and carry out a specific activity. Delegation is usually from one level on the organizational chart to a lower one.

Delegation does not mean getting rid of the jobs that you don't want to do. It means determining the best person for the job and giving that person the responsibility and authority to do it. Clearly you need to know the strengths and weaknesses of the people with whom you are working, and you need to use these to your best advantage. If you are loathe to delegate, then you need to examine your own motivation and consider why you have difficulty giving up specific tasks. A manager who cannot delegate will have significant operational and staff problems.

Delegation, however, also means that you need a regular means to communicate with these people on an ongoing basis so that you can maintain control of the project without taking away a certain degree of autonomy. Regular team meetings can be helpful, but individual meetings are also useful in maintaining control. Most management textbooks devote a significant amount of time to the skill of delegation. Refer to the reading list for more information.

Using the worksheets

There are three worksheets for this chapter. They are designed to assist you in managing the three most common managerial parameters – financial resources, time, and quality.

Use the first worksheet – the **Budgeting Worksheet**– to assist you in the first stages of planning for allocation of the financial resources for the project. In section 1, identify those individuals within your organization who will be charged with various specific responsibilities for this project. Begin with your own activities, your hourly rate, the projected number of hours you will spend and determine the total cost of your services. Then repeat this process for every individual who will be involved. Remember to include clerical, administrative, and other technical support.

Section 2 of the budget worksheet requires you to consider all outside services that this project will necessitate. Here you would consider printing, photography, courier, studio rentals, catering and the like. Before you can estimate these costs though, you'll need actual estimates from each of these people. You might even have requested such estimates from more than one source to ensure the best price.

Section 3 is where you list the materials that will be required for this project. If you are planning an event, for example, you'll need to consider every small detail such as name tags, pencils for the delegates, and markers for the flipcharts (unless the venue provides these – but you'll need to know). Also include an amount for out-of-pocket expenses – everyone forgets small things such as parking for the guest speaker from time to time!

The second worksheet is like a traditional Gantt chart for **Time Management**. Follow the instructions in the left-hand column and remember to revise your time management chart as the project progresses. Even if you don't always prepare a chart like this for implementation, it is a useful exercise to do it once in a while to ensure that you are still able to break down an activity into its constituent tasks and to estimate the time it will take for completion of each.

The final worksheet to use during the implementation phase, is the **Quality Control Checklist**. You may need to use more than one of these to assess the quality of specific aspects of the plan.

Budgeting Worksheet

Section 1 - Activities & Person Hours

Activity	Responsibility	Rate	Hours	Total

Total projected cost person hours _____

Section 2 - Outside Services

Description	Cost

Total projected cost outside services _____

Section 3 - Materials

Description	Cost

Total projected cost materials _____

GRAND TOTAL _____

Time Management

Gantt Chart

Activity

1. _____

2. _____

3. _____

4. _____

5. _____

6. _____

7. _____

8. _____

☐ Days   ☐ Weeks   ☐ Months   to completion

Instructions:

1. Prepare complete list of activities required to complete plan.

2. List activities as items on vertical axis.

3. Place an X at the time point where the activity must begin.

4. Place an X at the time point where the activity must end.

5. Join the Xs with a straight line.

5. Repeat for each activity (there will be time overlaps).

Quality Control Checklist

Consistency Measures

- ❑ messages consistent

- ❑ tone consistent

- ❑ style consistent

Reliability Measures

- ❑ each element moves toward overall goal

- ❑ elements together move toward organizational goals

Accuracy Measures

- ❑ content acurate

- ❑ materials error-free

Congruency Measures

- ❑ elements all "fit"

Honesty Measures

- ❑ message content truthful

- ❑ message delivery not misleading

Chapter 5

Evaluation

Vocabulary

- ☐ measurement
- ☐ quantitative
- ☐ qualitative
- ☐ media monitoring
- ☐ benchmarking
- ☐ reputation

A practical definition

Evaluation is both an ending and a beginning. Although this phase seems to bring up the rear of the four steps in the public relations process (research, plan, implement, evaluate), it should also be considered a beginning. And as such, it is arguably the most important step.

> Evaluation is a measurement of an organization's success in disseminating planned messages to its targeted publics to reach specific communication and relationship goals and objectives.

Thus, the data collected in an effort to measure the success or failure of any aspect of a public relations campaign or program are analyzed to provide useful information during the research phase of the next part of the program. It's like a circular feedback loop.

This chapter is about how to plan for evaluation of the public relations project. For more detailed information regarding how to carry out any of the specific types of evaluation strategies, you'll need to refer to the reading list at the end of the book (although many strategies are quite self-evident and need no special skills). The evaluation, then, is planned at the time that the project itself is planned, and it is only as valid as the objectives. We'll come back to this as we discuss the validity and complexity of what is often evaluated in public relations practice.

Although we tend to discuss evaluation as if it had its own discrete phase in the process, the reality of practice is that it is both terminal as well as ongoing. As we discussed in the last chapter, managing the implementation of the public relations project requires the manager to maintain some level of control over the activities and outcomes. The only way to do this is to consider ongoing evaluation to avoid surprises in the end. Some of the outcomes that can be measured as part of a summative evaluation can also be part of the ongoing evaluation as we discuss later.

Why evaluate?

Historically, public relations has been known by what people can actually see – what is implemented. The fact that what is implemented needs to be evaluated might seem self-evident in this age of accountability, but it is still not a foregone conclusion that everyone sees the need to evaluate what public relations does. Many people who are not schooled in the field seem to feel that a "gut" reaction is sufficient. Modern public relations and business practices take issue with that unsubstantiated approach.

Several years ago, a guest speaker in one of my first-year public relations classes presented a case study of a public relations campaign that had been implemented by the department of which he was a part. Much to these neophyte students' delight, he presented all of the print materials that had been used to disseminate a very well-thought-out message to a very specific target public. When asked about the success of the program, he happily reported that it had been a bang-up success. I thought of this as a good opportunity for students to see evaluation in action, so I asked him to tell the students how they had determined the success of the program. He said, "Everyone liked the posters!"

If the objective of the communications exercise had been to have everyone like the posters, then one would have no choice but to deem it a success. The objectives, however, would have been flawed and thus the outcomes just as flawed from a public relations perspective. This, however, is what I've come to term the happiness index, and it isn't nearly as extinct as an evaluation tool as it ought to be.

We need to evaluate public relations programs for many of the same reasons that we need to do research before we begin planning. The happiness index is not helpful.

What we evaluate

Just as in the selection of communication vehicles and channels, the selection of evaluation techniques and tools offers an opportunity for creativity. This creativity, however, is always tempered by the constraints inherent in the objectives of the plan. Thus, the goal here is to select evaluation tools that will measure *exactly what you intend to measure* in the public in which you intend to measure it.

Through the years, public relations managers have taken a variety of approaches to evaluation, not all of them useful, as we already have alluded to. Before you can create an evaluation plan, you need to consider the possibilities of what can actually be measured, how valid that measurement will be, and the feasibility of you being able to carry out the particular evaluation process.

What you evaluate is as telling about your professional judgment as your ability to select effective communication vehicles and approaches.

Here are some of the aspects of the public relations program that can be measured.

- how productive you've been
- how far afield you've disseminated your message(s)
- the accuracy of the message(s) disseminated
- whether anyone in your target public saw/heard the message
- change in knowledge level of your target public
- change in attitude of your target public
- change in behavior of your target public
- change in the quality of the relationship between this public and your organization.

Let's examine each of these in more detail so that you will be able to consider whether or not you would select a tool based on one of these general approaches.

How productive you've been: This is easy. If you want to know how productive you've been, you simply keep a tally of the work that's done during the implementation phase of the project. How many news releases did you write? How many interviews did you arrange? How many press conferences took place? Although there may be a good reason for keeping track of your productivity in this way (to bill clients, for example), there is little justification for using any of these approaches to evaluate the public relations project. This approach lacks validity in that it does nothing to measure communication/relationship outcomes at all. Just because you did a lot of work, does not necessarily translate into an effective or even efficient public relations campaign.

How far afield you've disseminated your message(s): Again, this is easy to track. How many media outlets received and used your news releases? How many brochures did you put in the mail? Where were they sent? Whereas this may seem like a step forward from simply counting your productivity, again it lacks validity as it does not measure communication effects, unless, of course, publicity is all you are looking for. The extent to which your message is exposed to people in general is an outdated way of looking at the effects of the public relations effort. Media monitoring seems to be one of most widely used tracking methods for public relations departments, but again it lacks validity in terms of what you really need to accomplish in terms of your relationships – with one possible exception. If you are working toward enhancing your organization's reputation with the media, you might be concerned that they begin to actually use your material. Keep in mind, however, that extrapolating to how many members of other publics saw and understood your message is dangerously lacking in substance. But there are also other reasons for doing media monitoring on a regular basis. We'll examine these later.

The accuracy of your message: Now we're beginning to look more at the qualitative aspect of the outcomes, rather than simply the quantitative aspects of the work that's been done. Assessing message accuracy in this way usually refers to the use of uncontrolled media. In other words, when you are using controlled media, the accuracy of the message is controlled by you at an earlier stage in the public relations process. On the other hand, the accuracy of the messages disseminated through mass media, for example, cannot be measured until it's really too late to do much about it. Thus, media monitoring that includes content analysis is useful and essential to an ongoing evaluation. Simply measuring the extent to which they "got it right" though, is again not a real communication effect, but a *process* effect.

Whether or not anyone in your target public saw or heard the message that you actually sent: This can be a useful way to evaluate the appropriateness of your selected channels and vehicles. It is necessary to find a way to ask members of your specific target public if they heard or saw your messages, and if they heard or saw them accurately. This, however, does not measure response.

Change in knowledge level of your target public: They say that knowledge is power and so it would seem that developing a communication program to enhance a public's knowledge level about your organization or issue is a powerful communication outcome. It can be, but it isn't necessarily. Clearly, an enhancement of a public's knowledge as a result of successful message dissemination is a positive outcome. Before we consider why it might not be the appropriate ultimate outcome that you need to measure the success or failure of your campaign, let's consider a public information campaign where the communication outcome that you want to achieve is, indeed, an increase in knowledge level.

In assessing the outcome of a public information campaign, whether it focuses on the prevention of skin cancer or on the nutritional aspects of dairy products, measurement of knowledge level is a valid way to evaluate the degree of success. How you carry out that evaluation accurately, however, is a complex issue. First, it's necessary to have an accurate picture of your target public's level of knowledge about the subject before the communication campaign begins. This may require what researchers call a **pretest-posttest design**. This technique involves assessing knowledge level before the application of the messages, and then after the campaign is complete to make comparisons. To do this accurately involves the use of scientifically designed surveys, which requires a high level of knowledge about research methods and can be expensive.

It's important to point out that whereas knowledge may be a substantial first step in the development of sound relationships with your organization's publics, it's highly likely that even this kind of accurate measurement of knowledge outcomes doesn't really get to the heart of what you want to achieve. To do that you need to consider the attitude, behavior, and relationship changes that you're really looking for.

Change in attitude and behavior of your target public:
The most powerful changes a public relations campaign can facilitate in a target public are changes in attitude (which can lead to expression of those changed attitudes or what we know as public opinion), and behavior. Consider a communication campaign about AIDS targeted at university-aged students. If the only communication outcome from the campaign is an increase in the students' knowledge level about AIDS and HIV infection, then the campaign is really only partially effective. What such a campaign really should be looking for is changes in attitude that have the potential to have a positive effect on how these students treat people with HIV infection, and a change in their personal behavior that might lead to a decrease in the number of times they put themselves at risk. In this kind of situation, however, the only way to measure a change in behavior is to ask.

There are other instances in public relations where the change in behavior might be measured more objectively. The plan may be designed to support sales and thus increased consumer spending on particular items would be useful behavioral measures. A plan designed to recruit volunteers would look at the actual numbers of volunteers. A plan to support corporate sponsorship would measure financial gains in sponsorship. The advantage of behavior measurement is that it is concrete and thus a valid measure of public relations outcomes. The problem is that the actual issue may be more esoteric.

For example, if the plan focuses on employee relations and deals with a problem of employees not seeming to respect and support one another, you may have to be more creative to find a way to measure an improvement in respect. You can hardly measure the amount of respect. But you might be able to keep track of employee involvement in a particular project that requires them to utilize one another's skills. As the public relations practitioner, it's your job to design that project.

Change in quality of the relationship:
This is at the heart of public relations and warrants its own discussion in the next section.

Evaluating relationships

At the heart of public relations is the focus on the development and maintenance of mutually beneficial relationships between organizations and their important publics. Although the foregoing discussion of the communication outcomes we can reasonably measure are useful in the measurement of direct communication outcomes, there is more to evaluation. The problem is: How do you measure something that is as seemingly intangible as a "relationship" between two entities?

In chapter 3, in our discussion of the planning phase of the public relations process, we considered the issue of relationship objectives. If you have developed specific objectives related to the degree of trust that the publics have for the organization, the extent to which they feel positively disposed toward the organization's products/services, policies, and activities, and the extent to which the publics feel that the organization gives back to then, them you also need to determine a way to measure these aspects of the relationship.

Some concrete examples of methods that you might use to gather data about the quality of the relationship include the following:

- opinion surveys conducted by the organization
- opinion surveys conducted by independent third parties
- focus groups
- hotline feedback
- community participation in organizational events
- media monitoring (limited and indirect, but useful)

What is important in the application of any of these evaluation strategies is the quality and content of the questions posed in the instruments. You can refer to the more in-depth materials suggested in the resource section for suggestions about the development of these materials.

In the end, the relationships that an organization has with its important publics are reflected in its reputation, and reputation is really nothing more than public perception of the organization. Reputation, however, is a key asset to the ability of any organization – not-for-profit, profitmaking or government – to flourish. Thus, considering the outcomes of any public relations activities on relationships is at the heart of evaluation.

Before we complete our discussion of evaluation, there is one more evaluation-related business concept that is worth discussing. That is the issue of benchmarking. Depending on where you do your reading about benchmarking, you may find one of several different takes on a definition.

The "benchmark"

In general, a benchmark is a standard against which you may compare or judge something.

Some people use the word to refer to the practice of seeking out how the successful competition does what they do, and setting that up as the standard against which your organization can compare itself. In the field of public relations, this kind of a benchmark is very difficult to obtain. This is at least partly a result of the fact that much of what public relations accomplishes seems intangible (a good argument for making your evaluation plan as tangible as possible).

Another way of looking at benchmarking is somewhat more useful in the evaluation of the public relations effort. This involves using your own public relations efforts of the past as standards against which you'll measure the outcomes of the future. Clearly, this involves the ongoing collection of data for comparison, and regular auditing of the ongoing public relations program, in addition to the more short-term campaigns.

In any case, the contribution that public relations projects make to the bottom line of any organization – whether for-profit, not-for-profit, or government – must be evaluated on a regular basis.

Using the worksheets

The final worksheet included here is a **Media Monitoring Tracking Sheet**. Every organization that does media monitoring has its own version of this form. It is included not because it's the most reliable way to measure the success of public relations (far from it, as we have already discussed), but it is an activity that most organizations ought to be doing on a regular basis. Adapt it to your own particular setting and use it daily.

Media Monitoring Tracking Sheet

Date	Medium[1]	Location	Direction[2]	Description	Initiated In-house[3]

[1] T = television
R = radio
N = newspaper
M = magazine

[2] + = positive
- = negative
N = neutral

[3] Y = yes
N = no

Resources

The suggested resources that follow are organized to provide you with additional information relating to each specific chapter. This is a workbook: It does not pretend to provide the background theory and practice base that a professional public relations practitioner ought to have to provide clients and employers with optimal public relations programming.

If, however, you wish to enhance your skills, the resources presented here will help you to think a bit more critically about what you do and what you see other public relations managers doing with their projects.

In addition, it is important to remember that there is more than one way to interpret and apply the public relations process. Consulting a variety of academic and industry resources will allow you to see different ways of viewing the same process.

Chapter 1

The readings and web resources selected to enhance the introductory chapter include a range of well-known, general textbooks in public relations as well as selected articles from both trade publications and academic journals on the general subject of what public relations is. The textbooks also include varying approaches to the 4-step public relations process. Some of the older references are now considered to be classics.

Baskin, O., Aronoff, C., & Lattimore, D. (1997). *Public relations: The profession and the practice* (4th ed.). Madison, WI: Brown & Benchmark.

Blewett, S. (1993, August). Who do people say we are? *Communication World*, 13-16.

Brody, W. (1992, Winter). The domain of public relations. *Public Relations Review*, 349-365.

Cutlip, S., Center, A., & Broom, G. (2000). *Effective public relations*. Upper Saddle River, NJ: Prentice-Hall.

Harlow, R. (1976, Winter). Building a public relations definition. *Public Relations Review, 2*, 34-42.

Hendrix, J. (1998). *Public relations cases* (4th ed.). Belmont, CA: Wadsworth.

Kendall, R. (1996). *Public relations campaign strategies: Planning for implementation* (2nd ed.). New York: Harper Collins.

McElreath, M. (1993). *Managing systematic and ethical public relations*. Madison, WI: Brown & Benchmark.

Newsom, D., Vanslyke Turk, J., & Kruckeburg, D. (1996). *This is PR: The realities of public relations* (6th ed.) Belmont, CA: Wadsworth.

Seitel, F. (1995). *The practice of public relations* (6th ed.). Englewood Cliffs, NJ: Prentice-Hall.

Sparks, S. (1993, Fall). Public relations: Is it dangerous to use the term? *Public Relations Quarterly*, 27-28.

Spicer, C. (1993). Images of public relations in the print media. *Journal of Public Relations Research, 5*, 47-61.

Wilcox, D., Ault, P., & Agee, W. (1998). *Public relations: Strategies and tactics* (5th ed.). New York: Addison Wesley.

The following resources provide both food for thought about how research fits into the public relations process, as well as much needed details about how to carry out research. Anyone who will be engaged in carrying out in-depth research, especially formalized processes such as surveys or focus groups, needs to study further to develop knowledge and skills. In addition, researchers need a much more focused knowledge in statistical procedures.

Chapter 2

Babbie, E. (1990). *Survey research methods* (2nd ed.). Belmont, CA: Wadsworth.

Barzun, J. & Graff, H. (1992). *The modern researcher* (5th ed.). Fort Worth, TX: HBJ College Publications.

Broom, D. & Dozier, D. (1990). *Using research in public relations*: *Applications to program management*. Englewood Cliffs, NJ: Prentice-Hall.

Dozier, D. (1985, Summer). Planning and evaluation in PR practice. *Public Relations Review*, 21-25.

Fahey, L. & King, W. (1977, August). Environmental scanning for corporate planning. *Business Horizons*, 47-51.

Geddie, T. (1996, April). Surveys are a waste of time...until you use them. *Communication World*, 24-26.

Grunig, L. (1990, Summer). Using focus group research in public relations. *Public Relations Review*, 36-49.

Ledingham, J. & Bruning, S. (1998-1999, Winter). Ten tips for better focus groups. *Public Relations Quarterly*, 25-28.

Lindenmann, W. (2001). *Let's put meaning into public relations research*. Institute for Public Relations Monographs. Retrieved 10/18/2002, from http://www.instituteforpr.com/researching.phtml

Nasser, D. (1988, March). How to run a focus group. *Public Relations Journal*, 33-34.

Pavlik, J. (1987). *Public relations: What research tells us*. Beverly Hills, CA: Sage.

Simpson, A. (1993, Summer). Ten rules of research: Meaningful, cost-effective research for PR programs. *Public Relations Quarterly*, 20-23.

Stolz, E. & Torobin, J. (1991, January). Public relations by the numbers. *American Demographics*, 42-46.

Chapter 3

A great deal of information about planning the public relations project is located in the general public relations textbooks listed under chapter 1 readings. The following provide some additional information and perspectives about the planning phase.

Dozier, D., Grunig, J. & Grunig, L. (1995). *Manager's guide to excellence in public relations and communication management.* Hillsdale, NJ: Lawrence Erlbaum Associates.

Frietag, A. (1998, Spring). PR planning primer: Bite-sized morsels make it simple. *Public Relations Quarterly*, 14-17.

Grunig, J. & Hon, L. (1999). *Guidelines for measuring relationships.* Institute for Public Relations Monographs. Retrieved 1/18/2002, from www.instituteforpr.com/relationships.phtml

Herrington, J. (1999, March). Bells and whistles are OK, but facts are better. *Communication World*, 23-25.

Lilienthal, P. (1998, February-March). Help management really communicate. *Communication World*, 19-22.

Pendleton, S. (1999, Spring). "Man's most important food is fat:" The use of persuasion techniques in Proctor and Gamble's PR campaign to introduce Crisco, 1911-1913. *Public Relations Quarterly*, 6-14.

Chapter 4

There is a wealth of information written about management in general. To find out more about the history of management and general management principles, any good management textbook aimed at a broad business audience will be useful. The following materials are selected to focus you in the direction of managing public relations projects.

Center, A. & Jackson, P. (1995). *Public relations practices: Managerial case studies and problems* (5th ed.). Englewood Cliffs, NJ: Prentice-Hall.

Forbes, P. (1992). Applying strategic management to public relations. *Public Relations Journal, 248 (3)*, 31-32.

Grunig, J. (Ed.). (1992). *Excellence in public relations and communications management.* Hillsdale, NJ: Lawrence Erlbaum Associates.

Hainsworth, B. & Wilson, L. (1992). Strategic program planning. *Public Relations Review, 18* (1), 9-15.

Managing corporate communications in a competitive climate. (1993). New York: The Conference Board.

Simmons, R. (1990). *Communication campaign management: A systems approach.* New York: Longman.

Warner, H. (1993). Working to establish public relations as a strategic management tool. *Public Relations Journal, 49 (4)*, pp. 18-23.

White, J. & Mazur, L. (1995). *Strategic communications management: Making public relations work.* Wokingham, England: Addison-Wesley.

Chapter 5

Again, you may want to read about evaluation in the general management literature, but here are some selected resources about evaluation in public relations. Some of these will give you more detailed information about the "how-to" of some evaluation tools.

Flesch, R. (1951). *How to test readability.* New York: Harper & Row.

Freitag, A. (1998, Summer). How to measure what we do. *Public Relations Quarterly*, 42-47.

Hauss, D. (1993, February). Measuring the impact of public relations. *Public Relations Journal*, 14-21.

Lindenmann, W. (1993, Spring). An effectiveness yardstick to measure public relations success. *Public Relations Quarterly*, 3-16.

Lindenmann, W. (1998-1999, Winter). Measuring relationships is key to successful public relations. *Public Relations Quarterly*, 18-24.

McElreath, M. (1977, Winter). Public relations evaluative research: Summary statement. *Public Relations Review, 3*, 21-38.

Paine, K. (1994, June/July). Move over TQM! Benchmarking is the new tool for the 90's. *Communication World*, 42-44.

Pretzer, M. (1994, November). How to measure your newsletter effectiveness. *Public Relations Tactics*, 8.

Public Relations Plan:
Sample Format

organization/client logo if desired

Name and Address of Organization/Client
Date

Prepared by:
project planning team members' names

Table of Contents

Purpose Statement

State the purpose of this document and who prepared it. This is also the place to explain the public relations terminology that you may be using throughout the plan. Not every client/employer will understand even the PR meaning of the term "publics," for example.

Executive Summary

Give a brief, concise summary of the strategy that follows.

Summarize the public relations problem(s) or opportunity(ies), delineate the overall goal of the plan, summarize the specific objectives, delineate key publics and why you have selected the priorities. Summarize the messages and highlight the key communications vehicles recommended in the plan. Finally, summarize how and why this plan will be evaluated. If you think it would be helpful, subheadings may be used in the executive summary.

This is a summary, not an introduction. It should be limited to two pages. When the summary is complete, begin the body of the plan on a new page.

Organizational Background

In this section you'll give an overview of the client. Provide basic information about the organization's name and location in this introduction. Describe the nature of the business and what kind of business it is (partnership, private, public, whatever).

History, Mission, & Structure

Begin with a statement about the origins of the organization. Then provide the mission statement and reference to any other important guiding principles that help to understand the function and direction of the organization. The organizational chart and a brief narrative explanation of it should also be included so that internal relationships may be delineated.

The structure and function of the public relations/communication role in the organization should also be presented here.

Environmental Pressures

This section provides a narrative description of the external environment within which the organization functions. It places the organization in the context of its overall industry and discusses the political, social, and economic pressures that play a part in the function of both the industry in general and this organization in particular. After the narrative description, the pressures or emerging issues are summarized in a list.

Public Relations/Communications Analysis

Introduction to the Analysis

This introduction explains how the data were collected and what sources were used in the ensuing analysis of communications/public relations issues. If this is a very large plan, a list of interviewees as well as the instruments used to collect data should be included in the appendix. In addition, a data analysis table may be included in the appendix.

Also included here are explanations of any limitations or delimitations on the data collection process and the time frame during which the analysis occurred.

Internal Publics

This section begins with an explanation of the importance of internal constituencies to this particular organization. A description of the organizational culture observed as well as reference to the data that support this observation is included here. This introduction is followed by a description of each important public identified during the data collection and a description of that public's relationship with the organization. This is not merely a listing, but a detailed description of the public. Subheadings are used to identify each public.

External Publics

This section is similar to the foregoing, but focuses on external publics– their characteristics and their relationship with the focal organization. These two groupings of publics are generic and somewhat arbitrary. Under certain circumstances, the publics should be categorized differently. For example, when creating a plan to address a controversial issue, rather than dividing the publics generally into internal and external groups, the broad groupings would include proponents, opponents, and neutral publics.

These external publics emerge partly as a result of your previous discussion of the external environment and partly from the organization's mission.

Strengths & Weaknesses

This is the narrative description of the data table that you may include in the appendix. It analyzes the current state of the communications and relationships between the organization and its currently identified publics. It also takes into consideration the current situation regarding the public relations management within the organization concluding with a list of strengths and a list of weaknesses in communications and relationships.

Public Relations Problems & Opportunities

From the strengths and weaknesses previously identified, some problems and opportunities become evident. Strengths generally give rise to opportunities on which the organization can capitalize, whereas weaknesses help to identify problems that require solutions. A priority problem/opportunity may also be identified.

Publics, Objectives & Messages

The Strategic Goal

The strategic goals is a specific statement of the overall goal that this strategic public relations plan will address. Specifying this relies on the accurate identification of problems and opportunities. The goal should be a brief (up to 25 words or so) statement that includes a broad reference to the public or publics involved so that these may be further segmented as necessary.

Identification of Priority Publics

After the data have been explained in the descriptions of the publics, this section begins the analysis. The reason for selection of the priorities is provided and then the priority publics that will be addressed in this strategic plan are identified in rank order. If this is a multiyear plan, priorities for each year are identified.

Strategic Objectives

Strategic objectives are those outcomes toward which this plan will strive for each priority public. Because some of the objectives will overlap one or more publics, these outcome objectives may either be provided for each individual public or for specific groupings. For example, the outcome objectives may be the same for all internal publics

Core Message

It is important to be specific and to provide a succinct statement that encapsulates the overall strategic message. This message should underlie any messages that are communicated by both word, tone, and deed in the strategy to achieve the strategic goal.

Strategic Approaches

This section describes exactly what approaches the organization will take to meet the specific objectives set out previously for each public. There are various approaches to presenting these. However, keying these strategies to the objectives they are designed to achieve is key.

Strategies & Rationales

Not only are the strategies described (e.g. an event, print publication(s), the development of an award, a community activity, new media policies, media training for executives, a web-based strategy, implementation of a hotline etc.), but rationales are provided. Why was this approach selected? How do we know that it is likely to have the desired effects?

These proposed approaches are described in as much detail as possible. The following questions must be answered:

- What is planned?
- When will the development take place?
- When will it be completed?
- Who will do what parts of it?
- How much will it cost in terms of resources and money?
- What will it look like?
- Why are you proposing this strategy?

Time Line and Budget

This is a summary of the time and budgetary considerations presented in the previous section. Some kind of time management tool and budget sheet are included in the appendix.

7

Evaluation Strategies

Evaluation and Rationales

Each strategy proposed in the previous section needs to be evaluated in terms of the objectives it was designed to achieve.

This section answers the question: How will we know if the strategy was successful and how will we measure it? It also addresses the issue of why a particular evaluation strategy is proposed. Ensure that both communication and relationship outcomes are included if applicable in this plan.

If data collection is indicated (such as media monitoring), the plan needs to provide an instrument for this purpose. The instrument itself is placed in the appendix.

Appendices

Samples of inclusions in the appendices:

- Data sources for the analysis (list of who was interviewed, etc.)
- Interview guidelines
- Data table
- Resources required for implementation
- Budget
- Time management materials (e.g. a Gantt chart)
- Samples of evaluation tools
- Sample template for print publication or any other tools proposed

About the Author

An Associate Professor & past-chairman of the four-year Bachelor of Public Relations degree program at Mount Saint Vincent University in Halifax, Nova Scotia, Canada, Patricia Parsons currently teaches managing organizational public relations and communication planning, as well as the senior course in public relations ethics. Prof. Parsons has overseen the development of over 500 strategic plans for students who produce these for actual clients as part of their course requirements.

A medical communication specialist by background, since 1988 Prof. Parsons has been a medical writer for both the professional, academic and lay press, in Canada and the U.S. In addition to feature writing for a variety of trade and industry publications, she is the author or co-author of six previous books on health, ethics and communication.

Her most recent book *Beyond Persuasion: Strategic Communication for Healthcare Managers* was released in 2001 by Health Administration Press, Chicago. She maintains a consulting practice at *Biomedical Communications Incorporated* focussing on strategic communication planning for health and human service organizations as well as professional development of communication and writing skills for managers.